MIGRATORY SOUND

CANTO MUNDO
POETRY SERIES
EDITED BY CAROLINA EBEID
AND CARMEN GIMÉNEZ SMITH

Migratory Sound

~ POEMS ~

Sara Lupita Olivares

The University of Arkansas
Fayetteville
2020

ISBN: 978-1-68226-149-1
eISBN: 978-1-61075-731-7

Manufactured in the United States of America

24 23 22 21 20 5 4 3 2 1

Designed by Liz Lester

⊗ The paper used in this publication meets the minimum requirements of
the American National Standard for Permanence of Paper for Printed Library
Materials Z39.48-1984.

Library of Congress Cataloging-in-Publication Data
Names: Olivares, Sara Lupita, author.
Title: Migratory sound / poems.
Description: Fayetteville: The University of Arkansas Press, 2020. |
  Series: Cantomundo poetry series | Summary: "In its various terrains
  and habitats, Migratory Sound glances back to generational narratives of
  immigration, moving from south to north exploring seasonal field work
  and factory labor. By looking to ancestral narratives of Mexican American
  immigrants, the poems examine spatial and geographic boundaries and
  linguistic and mental intersections"—Provided by publisher.
Identifiers: LCCN 2020010068 (print) | LCCN 2020010069 (ebook) |
  ISBN 9781682261491 (paperback; alk. paper) | ISBN 9781610757317 (ebook)
Subjects: LCGFT: Poetry.
Classification: LCC PS3615.L57 M54 2020 (print) | LCC PS3615.L57 (ebook)
  | DDC 811/.6—dc23
LC record available at https://lccn.loc.gov/2020010068

LC ebook record available at https://lccn.loc.gov/2020010069

for Ramona

Contents

Series Editors' Preface

Of Sara Lupita Olivares's *Migratory Sound,* series judge Roberto Tejada writes:

> This is a rare, evocative, and haunting book. For its sparse song of indwelling in landscapes of austerity; for its understanding of description as a function subordinate to wakefulness of mind, for its process of perception that splits the difference between animal and oblivion, habit and habitat, doubt and debt—I found myself returning again and again to its atmospheric method of knowing; to its structure of restraint and elegance.

You will notice the book is full of traces, of the faint vestige of something removed. Whether enacting a bird migration, or the uprooting of people relocating north, or the private movement from sleep to alert vigilance, Olivares's stark poetry concerns the precarious idea of place and its underlying "unplace." She makes evident how every place bears a relationship with an elsewhere, an *over there* sometimes situated underneath: "in the field there is another field chewed down / until motionless. how the private disfigures / the external." Her spare poems unsettle with murmurs, hisses, and chirps.

Olivares offers a poetry resonant with that of the Argentinian poet Alejandra Pizarnik. There is a nebulous weather inside the intellect at work here, heavy with motion, the way clouds shift and churn, an intellect with the ardor for abstraction swiftly cut by the sharp edge of an image, in the manner of an airplane descending through the overcast. As in Pizarnik's work, what burdens these poems into being is the need to communicate with the language of "a broken jaw / reassembled"; the poems in these pages are "giving sun / its gold torn speak."

It is then fitting that *Migratory Sound* begins at night when darkness charges the landscape, recasting what was familiar in the daylight into something more peculiar: "dead animals on / the road begin to change the way color dims / you from a place." Such estrangements span the length of Olivares's work, whose speaker commands your attention, though not with a loud, formidable voice, but with a hushed timbre that you will find yourself leaning in to hear. Listening itself becomes a mode of travel through the work; the poems assemble into soundscapes wherein the reader encounters many animal noises: "it is not a mistake when the rustling quiets and then stops. the animal remains / hidden." Even the poet's name stays obscured in plain sight: "*lupita* meaning little wolf."

Carolina Ebeid
Carmen Giménez Smith

Acknowledgments

Gratitude to the editors of the journals and chapbook in which versions of these poems have appeared: *Apogee*: "Openings"; *Columbia Poetry Review*: "Respond to View," "What Never Converges," "Moment Where I Keep What I'd Wanted to Give," and "Numbers"; *Denver Quarterly*: "Correspondence," "Etymology," and "Maps"; *DIAGRAM*: "Glimpse" and "Animalier: On Stasis"; *Gulf Coast: A Journal of Literature and Fine Arts*: "Where the Field Retracted" and "On Balance"; *Horse Less Review*: "About Oblivion," "Certain Noise," "Form," "Small Ghost," and "Toward"; *jubilat*: "Of Small Spaces"; *Newfound*: "Night"; *Salt Hill Journal*: "Collective" and "Drawn Animals"; *The Boiler Journal*: "Moment to Moment" and "Migratory Sound"; *The Cincinnati Review*: "Drawings of a Red-Billed Pigeon"; *The Florida Review Latinx/Latina/Latino Issue*: "Circuit"; *The Pinch Literary Journal*: "Against"; *Third Coast Magazine*: "Clarities"; *Verse Daily*: "Moment Where I keep What I'd Wanted to Give"; *Winter Tangerine*: "Of Inheritance" and "The Field as a Circle" (forthcoming); and *dancing girl press*: some of these poems appeared in my chapbook *Field Things*.

*

Thank you to CantoMundo for creating a space for Latinx writers, to Roberto Tejada for choosing this manuscript, and to Carolina Ebeid and Carmen Giménez Smith for first seeing these poems. To everyone at the University of Arkansas Press who has guided me. To each of my teachers in Michigan and Texas and specifically to those who helped me find these poems: Kathleen Peirce, Nancy Eimers, Cyrus Cassells, and Bill Olsen. To my Michigan and Texas poets who wrote along with me. To my family—for your love and for your belief. To Ramona Tula Conde who has always been with me: for your kindness, patience, curiosity, humor, and love. To Jason Legaspi Conde for wandering around with me, seeing awe with me, and for your love. To my grandmothers Ramona and Mary Clara: for your displacement, placement, stories, and secrets. To my family gone before the writing of this book and during: thank you for still being near.

MIGRATORY SOUND

NIGHT

before loss there is habit   the moon implied beyond a fence

outside a goat crosses the pavement
hooves circle in the snow   a broken jaw

reassembled   I begin to make a house despite the highway

what song into the child's ear subtracts an animal's
forage end to end   the wrong leaves have been

eaten   each absent correspondence bleats
you misinterpret the animal's mouth

as objectivity
each unparticular way of seeing

*

MOMENT WHERE I KEEP
WHAT I'D WANTED TO GIVE

once they appear
I reach out to touch
the minnows
a loose hinge of me
opens and closes
normally

I halve my life
to see how
want balances
want lessening
the light's
threads

ANIMALIER: ON STASIS

the figure of an animal does not pose.
        in its flux it is drawn in
silhouette, seen anatomical with loss of
           color, light, and movement.

    *

two peacocks facing away from one another.
        drawn without feathers as dead sparrows,
their tails mathematic. the similarities and differences
        meaning nothing, context worn away.

    *

when drawing the anatomy of a woman,
        da Vinci often used animals—the uterus of
a horse or bear. the oddly shaped light.

    *

to create an illusion the animal must
        remain anonymous.
in the field there is another field chewed down
        until motionless. how the private disfigures
the external. through distance a quiet hysteria becomes illogic.

WHERE THE FIELD RETRACTED

indifference requires a lineless sky

    the muted television appears

a substitution

what split from the body days ago

    still hovers in a corner

of the stairwell

    to sleep a position-less

    arc between

concept and illustration

waking slow to hail falling on the air unit

    any case of interiority

itself reversible

    arguably imagined

ETYMOLOGY

the ambitious wreck erases its reason
trees birds sea-
scapes

someone else's memory
reappears

though it is much smaller
than your own

OF SMALL SPACES

glass eye
    of a crow
salt grasses
wave by
    to instead
remain lost
    what washes up
explains survival
a note
    removed
from the forest empty
    elsewhere
smokestacks over town
    movement as a means
of obscuring
white field
    of roses
children in
a line
    how forage
diminishes form as
    observer the crow
avoids its
dead rerouting
    paths of hunger in
avoidance again and again
    held in
place
even when
    remaining still

MIGRATORY SOUND

it may have been a bone stuck in the throat

a painting of a meadow dead animals on

the road begin to change the way color dims

you from a place language practiced without

a terrain to think abstractly of one's body

tracing north to south and back again

* *

DRAWINGS OF A RED-BILLED PIGEON

you can see only the shape of the red-billed pigeon
       in the bathroom window, opaqueness
a distance the yard

repeats. the moon sinks—its
       persistence a syllable swelling
through the day.

a child draws worry as a river,
       its stones neatly pressed to one side.
when we take a photograph of the landscape

we find ghosts of trees in ways dimming
       around themselves to create
indentations of other selves.

I come home and empty out someone else's
       drawers. the blurriness of
trees deepens, though the periphery remains

pointed as if to highlight, interiority being
       a complicated resolve. the red-billed
pigeon halfway hatched from its egg

its shell a root taken from
       a landscape and turned upside
down, our own want left to

unplace its things within idled
       forms. you can hear a singing still before
opening—the self quietly separated from its own sound.

CORRESPONDENCE

in the diagram
we are
carried
off now
I describe
the flowers—
that *they flowered*
attaching themselves
blindly
to what was
the difficult
bright

GLIMPSE

it takes nothing—the many flowers beheaded, the grass empty
and uninhabited. transplanted, the roots hang anonymous and empty.

the letter begins in feigned humility. a wheel without spokes
radiates. the unseen value of timid sound, its response empty.

in the drawings of seas and mountains, a doe's spotted back
camouflaged. the sea nearly uprooted where rocks emerge and empty.

sometimes a person posed in a garden. the portrait peering back.
in other paintings the flowers are cut, placed in a vase, this movement empty.

the public and private conflated in a dream sequence. the sinew
of my own intrusion. we find the map, names scribbled, following, empty.

there is a complete list, and I wonder what occurs when order disappears
out of forgetfulness or in being diminished by wear. intention then empty.

surrender or lack of will in nature becomes unnoticeable in its disorder.
a perfectly intact bird dead under the dogwood, its shadow cast empty.

when bending the neck to drink from the river. when tilting the head back or
forward to sleep. the invisible navigation embedded, followed, empty.

it is not a mistake when the rustling quiets and then stops. the animal remains
hidden. *lupita* meaning little wolf. one's own habitat empty.

WHEN CONSIDERING THE WATER

to follow yourself into an unknowing

where a painting hovers in the mind

its light an arguable force reconciling

the body to the water as Bonnard's

nude in her bath becomes another

garden in scattered pattern

each plane a figureless

line lost entirely

CIRCUIT

somewhere a bough's shadow contradicts its shape

any instance and the ghost will unhinge its loneliness

where it recognizes its past in one version the pasture

is a complicated tradition where moss gathers on the roof

the mind sees a plain in another version the pasture

feels the doe's teeth in a forethought the many flowers

give where the seen and implied become patterned

another's currency is abstraction Victor's hand cut off

in a machine at the paper mill down the street each

morning the sulfuric air my inheritance is a dialogue of

transgressions the sound and shape of the landscape omitted

TO MAKE BEAUTY IN SOME SENSE IMPERISHABLE

moss circles the bough until it becomes consumed.

what beauty consoles the yellow leaves.

half rotted the short stalks bend. the half of

my body made of you remains speechless.

the sedge in a finch's mouth. where in the torso

guilt grows bone. small openings reveal nothing

but I press the parts into place until they become

formless and tilt away from conscience.

OF INHERITANCE

Because of the reckless woods
     what follows doesn't make the bird call back.

What in a private image remains unknown
     to even oneself.

Guadalupe hated the north because it was
     too *blanco* and she spoke little English.

Her children and their children a kind of muteness
     the weeds could retract.

Each small thing that vanishes
     takes up more space.

The tops of the pines point
     toward nothing. The mirror of non-identity

where shortfall is to fury as place
     is to self-silence.

THE FIELD AS A CIRCLE

how many boxes have you filled without thought.

a gray fish floats across the water. we tie the mattress

on top of the car and doubt that the plain feels fallowed.

how you negotiate yourself from place to place.

yellow light frames the landscape. a story begins

long ago. but the ground is colorless and vague.

what is underneath has been separated root from root.

exposure yields an unrequited falling away but to pull

the field bare no doubt committed to memory.

RESPOND TO VIEW

sews finish beginnings

watch a wall grow candle laughs

grace grows enduring threads

horizon's shadow marries soil

it is quail contrary and gray asps

it is sea contrary and furrowing

a height-raised impulse

to the bird giving sun

its gold torn speak

ON BALANCE

after blooming the cactus shrivels incrementally

*

driving away, an ox—its horns crooked

*

blame grows small in the moth's circling

*

day to day the slightest tooth loosens

*

a landscape changes until returning by habit

*

the child's sound repeats without concept

*

where intention collects—a sparrow lost in topiary

PASTORAL

within the pond there is an incidental pond

        a sheep's wool yellows and curls away from sun

     immobility becomes an act of reasoning

an orchid misplaced opens

        how a place comes to exist only in its repetition

     blue smokestacks in the periphery

        at night the woods call back their animals

each note errorless and audible

CLEMENCY

The swan hovers damply.
How much can anyone be but without
anyone knowing.

Without, I should have known and combed
the blonde mums
from the stairway.

MOMENT TO MOMENT

the appearance of a dark stain on the ceiling
        is a symbol that makes its perceiver
become a symbol
        its presence colors out
where violet weeds grow near an underpass
        I watch my daughter by the road
with a different sense
of violence
        the way a cloud when depicted
on television seems small in its detachment
        from reality
and want in that space to know a figure
        in its harmless entirety

FERTILITY

there were fleets of swans

in their slow steps

crossing a frozen lake

the vague directions

I lost my keys

is this luxury or luxurious

I have such patience

FORM

why did the wood dove because

of its particular affirmation tilted

wanting to see the gutters wanting

to know whether it was the orange

garage peeling or the mosquito

netted in light its tedious arch

being midday light holding

your hair and your tired

center the ordinary

grass swayed

to bits

STATIC

the cattle dehorned and faced from the windows

in the long hours the moon pales

daylight sometimes a residue

the unintentional figure made in waiting

to sometimes ask to rehearse a story another repeats

made in idleness retracing the distance

ON REMOTENESS

I fall asleep in a dream as if watching
the grid pile image into transparency

over the gray surface swans move into
a secondary occurrence

shifting outward their bodies become
another material repeated disfiguring

****

IMPLIED SURROUNDINGS

two dogs appear out of the snow
if the body, the wallpaper repeating

if the mind, fruit in grass and opening
the landscape is an opaqueness

less in the sense of muting—instead a blankness
presses out from how light

opposes gravity and describes
without

DRAWING OF A BEAR WALKING

a faint woman lies under the bear, its eyes

gaze past her. an ordinary garden splayed as if

the sun at times grows sightless. where two forms

overlap there is the bright incoherence of meaning.

the paper reused. the bear's paws a discourse

redrawn. stillness becomes an echo

negating itself with each instance.

MANIFEST

the dull brown eyes of an ox looking back / looking back /
        looking back / looking back

        *

*although my intellect in its simplicity and ignorance
did not recognize the great defects in
myself and in others
it must nonetheless
be so.*

        *

to assume rational authority: Io in the dirt scraping her name.

        *

the theme of movement carries on throughout
Bonnard's paintings, fixated on steadiness and repetition.

a nude woman near the bath scrubbing or drying, hurtling
or recessing. caught in pattern for eternity.

SLEEPWALK

a. in her tulip gait
steps through
the yard, a red
thread stitched
into this image
walking
backward
to unwind

WHAT NEVER CONVERGES

memory sings to the cardinal
that carries its home inside its mouth

the elephant statue worries rectangular
having watched the meadow

crawl inward having watched
clover weed its bells
flower

we play house to learn
what else
to say

HINGE

Without, the fly
could not contemplate
anything.

No choice to lift, no choice to land.
The world a single
direction.

LIES ABOUT HORSES

My joy was a mare.
I will call you a mule.

I enunciate and it is poppies
replayed in the sink.

My mule, you are my mare.

WORN-YARD GAMES

Memory has a laugh.
It is a kite in a hare's lung.
a. is small. She sleeps
wrapped like a tulip.
We completely doubt
the gray figure in trees.
There is too much
it would have to imply.

SEASONS

everyone is lucky
  they are chewing
cherries out of the petaled refrigerator
     these cold teeth
     a hole in the dirt where a root is pulled
           our tolerance
         begun

NUMBERS

a. fell in snow.
Stood up
and counted
imaginary feet
to measure
her width.

Fish swung
under the
frozen lake.

The body's
intentional
everywhere
faints and blooms.

AGAINST

flightless winter has a reversing
too

the sea's open even parts

breaking in a tired
row

*

somewhere birds left far from theirs

sailors enforcing their own distance

sometimes it is a whole year I draw lines

into the water circling myself against

the landscape

*

a red shovel drags
revealing ice over the water

the stilled boat into the grass
each practicality of resembling

*

when the tree shook we
thought of the absence
of birds

on the couch the light revealed
anything the way we built ourselves into small
rooms and left ourselves improbably

HONORABLE WRECKAGE

I didn't want to but understood why I would.
Wisteria fights the house and I am unable
to understand something so perfectly furious.
Inside, ghosts gain courage. They ask permission
to touch my dishes, my faucets—things
they don't need. I give them permission.

TOWARD

obligatory orchids
wave
I crawl
under
the leaves
to understand
the garbage
what is anyone's
karma
besides a
misunderstanding

FOREST

sometimes an impersonal

paper birch

opens

resurrection as a sense

of direction

the air undone

the birds

held up

examined and on

their way

STAIRWAY

when water equates to minnows
equates to swimming up to the surface
thinking that the sun
is food

open your
mouth

CERTAIN NOISE

pines and meadows reason

fishermen dividing waters

age to deep boat ends

detachment is a quiet

crowd as much

as a remote

sweeping

RADIANT

the boat
wore me

like its crumpled
scale

that kept count
of days

luz y
luz
y luz

we had been
looking

for air

the entire
time

TINT

water catch a certain glass weather
whether anyone pleas
they drink enough
to taunt
a root

CLARITIES

under the moon a tide— fish eggs hatch
    in the reeds

a stone broken open reveals
    no gleam

out of one conversation three small accusations

while the plum's skin falls the flies
    pause and watch

a motionless lake—the moored bottom shifts

through hierarchy a sound quiets
    where leaves blow open, the wet dirt

a landscape without concurrence

having watched, the animal too
    buries its dead

COLLECTIVE

The birds highlight absence.

Similarly we make ourselves appear

as though illusory.

What does the body begin to owe.

Each debt it sinks

itself into.

PATTERN WITHOUT LINE

the mute swan catches in
    its own misunderstanding
the certainty of indifference
my own unguided
    lighting up
having little to do with

    *

it isn't a window where I look for you and plant
    bulbs but not wanting
this language
    the deer pull them back out of the dirt

    *

as if we could speak out of ourselves
    an intuitive body in debt
        I forget the illiterate sense
a yard indents because it has a thought
    which it appears absent against
this is the difference now

WHAT IS YOUR GRIEF

absence becomes the quietness taken in by trees

to make this into an unnoticeable sky

clouds disassemble and leave the periphery

ants crawl out of a hyacinth where is your belief

undone the motion tormented by the body

what is your clarity mother without

a nounless form

TO WATCH

somewhere a heron
lost from the sedge
traces its shadow
grass pressed into
the ground where
our language suggests
a body there is none

WITHIN HANDS

the disjointedness of line without pattern

spooled water under a faucet

what I breathe into another slips out of

to instead dream stillness backward

to instead peel away one by one

the small animal's burrs

ON FORGETTING

the same way
we forget birds
inside a field
in the small
space we are
not thinking
of ourselves
though explain
a sort of glad
displacement

WITHOUT VANISHING

to perceive, the viewer
    turns back
from the object

a landscape becomes
antiquity

our own peculiarities
most hidden

outside the frame there is
a shifting that begs
    correction

a wilderness in a succession
    of bright colored images

continually disappearing from
view

SMALL GHOST

the part that jars like a seed
from its shell
floats

as certain
as its victorian nightgown

everything similar and mahogany
each noise settling

someone singing

JAW IN GRASS

the mouth
opens

but its
weight

carries
thought

out of
the water

out by
its hair

a knowable
vein

becomes
a root

light
pulled

inward
against

the sunken
form

ABOUT OBLIVION

want lamps quiet

minds of white sails

birds tilted live fluid

I remember remembered

forgot

how love woke

looking

how bones deepen

animals

how we speculate

tragedy

speaking bright

into morning

MAPS

of this geometry

I began to think

the seaside

to my own

little fishes

in the cities built

I draw inside

some industrious

animal that beaks

beauty

all of these forests

turn in a spiral line

and could be

of no help

OPENINGS

a small animal
in your hands

gives one expression
the way trauma

deepens in its
ephemera

a type of awe
you can sometimes

peel back
to see yourself

renegotiated
& watching again

WHAT DO YOU SEE

I didn't do very well
at leaving the meadow.

The loud wasp
was a similar conversation

of letters on charts
contradicting color

to contradict color.

RESEMBLANCES

the cacti without

    sightline

        multiply weaving

    low between

           the maze of rocks

in another direction

        they are reduced

          to dove-gray

      skeletons

without ideology

    the light

        appears thrown

            away

at a glance

      dictated by nothing

DRAWN ANIMALS

a boat somewhere in the after-all

built beneath and certain the frozen

mountain certain the tired minnow

indents of blue map thick and side

to side the fruit dimmed in

like glass the order it takes

to disappear

Notes

"Drawings of a Red-Billed Pigeon" departs from an image and description in *Portraits of Mexican Birds* by ornithologist George Miksch Sutton and conservationist Enrique Beltrán.

"Manifest" uses language from Dorothy Wordsworth's *Grasmere Journals* in the first stanza; the second stanza includes lines from Christine de Pizan's *The Book of the City of Ladies*; and the last two stanzas gesture toward Pierre Bonnard's painting *Getting out of the Bath*.

"When Considering the Water" refers to Bonnard's painting *Nude in the Bath*.

"Drawing of a Bear Walking" is indebted to Leonardo da Vinci's sketch "A Bear Walking" and its accompanying museum label at the Metropolitan Museum of Art in New York City.

"Forest" includes lines from H. D.'s *Trilogy*.

"To Watch" uses language from Ludwig Wittgenstein's *Remarks on Color*.

"Resemblances" uses language from Rebecca Solnit's *Savage Dreams*.